CONCRETE ELEGANCE THREE

The **Concrete** Centre™

RIBA 🏛 **Publishing**

FOREWORD

Concrete Elegance is a showcase for innovative and creative concrete architecture, exemplified by the many exciting and diverse projects and products that are presented by architects and designers at The Building Centre.

This publication is the third in the series and considers both pigmented and natural concrete colours, and how concrete can be detailed to accommodate the variations in colour or left untreated with the marks of construction visible. The quality of the architecture has never been in doubt, as shown by the examples in this edition – the black concrete of the Utrecht Library, the grass-imprinted precast panels of the A16 Toll Booths in France, the pink glass reinforced concrete (GRC) panels of Villaverde in Madrid and the plain grey concrete in the Bacon Street House. Yet, somehow, the interpretation and end results of using tried and tested concrete mixes and commonly used forming materials still offer almost limitless design freedom and scope for expression.

The landscape, hardscape, parkland and playground projects and domestic artefacts reviewed in this edition also help to broaden our understanding of concrete's potential and universal appeal. It was fitting that the 2006 series finished with a celebration of the stunning Millau Viaduct crossing to coincide with the Building Centre's 75th anniversary.

We look forward to seeing you at the next series.

Allan Haines
Head of Education, The Concrete Centre

C

ACKNOWLEDGEMENTS

The Concrete Centre wishes to thank all the speakers for their contribution to the success of the 2006 series, and for helping with the supply of images and for assisting with notes for the drafting of this text.

For information on future Concrete Elegance events, please contact The Concrete Centre or The Building Centre Trust.

Written and edited by
David Bennett
David Bennett Associates

Booklet designed by
Kneath Associates

© The Concrete Centre 2007
Published by
RIBA Publishing
15 Bonhill Street
London EC2P 2EA

ISBN 978 1 85946 280 5

Stock Code 58499

RIBA Publishing is part of RIBA Enterprises Ltd
www.ribaenterprises.com

D

CONTENTS

CONCRETE ELEGANCE IS A SERIES OF ARCHITECTURAL PRESENTATIONS GIVEN AT THE BUILDING CENTRE BY LEADING DESIGNERS, INNOVATORS AND MANUFACTURERS OF CONCRETE. THESE WERE THE THEMES AND SUBJECTS OF THE 2006 SERIES.

E

CONCRETE ELEGANCE//
01OVERVIEW

It is self-evident that concrete is winning the hearts and minds of young architects today in much the same way that it once did as a new material in the 1930s. The projects in this publication confirm this to be a continuing trend, with imaginative and inspiring designs emerging and some breaking of new ground. High quality concrete products are also being developed for the domestic market in the shape of firebowls, and furniture with fabric-formed construction is being acknowledged as a new art form.

One of the recurring themes that threads its way through these essays and is evident on construction sites is the question of concrete colour and surface consistency. There are no hard and fast rules to fashion concrete architecture a particular way, other than being prescriptive and rigorous with the specification. David Chipperfield's two major projects in Spain show the contrast in finishes achieved, between the pink GRC panels of the Villaverde development in Madrid and the smooth, evenly coloured insitu finishes of the impressive City of Justice Buildings in Barcelona. Most concretes, especially those with high pigment dosages that are cast in place, tend to patinate and lighten in colour as the concrete dries out and carbonates. For the GRC panels, Chipperfield intelligently exploited this

condition to advantage by detailing the GRC panels with slightly different pigment concentrations. The overall effect is to liberate the solid monumental mass of the building. By contrast, the smooth, even concrete colour for the façades of the City of Justice Buildings was achieved using low pigment dosages and self-compacting concrete with high fines contents.

Architects Toumey and O'Donnell showed the craft and care of fine detailing for the board-marked concrete soffits of the Glucksman Gallery, as did architects Greenway and Lee working with a very modest budget on the Spedant Works project. The board marking was consistent and even in colour because of the quality of the timber and the concrete mix specified. At the other end of the scale, architect William Russell was neither anxious nor preoccupied about the concrete colour or the quality of the joinery used for his Bacon Street house, so long as the surface was hard and durable.

Two of Europe's most talented architects Wiel Arets and Manuelle Gautrand gave us hints about the future direction their architecture may take. The Library Building at Utrecht University with its 'floating' black concrete façade and the etched glass curtain wall defies categorisation. Wiel Arets tears

up the rule books to create sensitive and sensuous design, removing utility and ordinariness from his design vocabulary in delivering such well thought out architecture. Manuelle Gautrand is just as fearless in her design approach, and equally uninhibited by historical precedent or sentimentality in the execution of her ideas. The Motorway Toll Booths project on the A16 in northern France draws inspiration from the fields of corn, poppies and lavender that had to be excavated to build the motorway and exploits the tradition of stained glass for the canopy roof in a region that boasts some of the greatest gothic cathedrals in France.

The green dock in Thames Barrier Park by Patel Taylor brings landscape, greenery and concrete together in a subtle and invigorating combination, hinting at sustainability without preaching. The concrete retaining walls enclosing the green dock are covered with a privet hedge growing hard against the high walls, reabsorbing the CO_2 that was emitted by the cement embodied in the concrete perhaps! Landscape, concrete and play were also the dominant themes for Eger Architects' Adventure Playground design in south London. The 'armadillo' wall that stands 7m high and runs along the pavement edge frames the indoor climbing wall and administration offices.
It has a surface finish of indented cups created by

using a black plastic drainage membrane attached to the form face. Architects Janson and Wolfrum showed how they used white precast concrete slabs to create a natural cascade for the rainwater soakaways that form the 1,000m green spine of a new housing development near Stuttgart.

And, finally, to end the year and to celebrate The Building Centre's 75th anniversary, a presentation was given on the design overview of the stunning Millau Viaduct by Jean-Françoise Coste (CNISF), Alistair Lenczner (Foster and Partners) and Russell Stanley (PERI Ltd). They collectively highlighted the purpose of the 2.4km viaduct, the aesthetic design of the cable-stayed bridge and the construction of those astonishing tall concrete piers.

We hope you enjoy the edited highlights of this series of Concrete Elegance and that it may challenge and provoke you to take a closer look at concrete and to make your own mind up about its versatile and creative potential in every form of architecture.

David Bennett
June, 2007

CONCRETE ELEGANCE//
02LANDSCAPE, PLANTING AND HARDSCAPE

Landscape, Planting and Hardscape
Evergreen Concrete Ideas

Andrew Taylor, Patel Taylor Architects
Selina Dix-Hamilton, Eger Architects
Alban Janson, Janson and Wolfrum Architects, Stuttgart

The relationship between urban regeneration, landscape architecture and the imaginative use of public spaces has been very skilfully combined and contrasted in the architecture of these three public projects. They have one thing in common – an understanding of how to express and detail concrete in a landscape.

Thames Barrier Park, London Docklands
Andrew Taylor, Patel Taylor Architects

London's first major post-war park has been built over a 9 hectare brownfield site to create a rich and inviting public space and to provide settings for different activities. It was an initiative started by the London Docklands Development Corporation (LDDC) to bring value into the area and to complement the residential buildings that have mushroomed around the park.

The aerial view of the site showed the vastness of its man-made dockland topography. Between the river edge and the main road there was an existing 5m drop, with the road being the lowest point. This was created when the docks were first dug out to form bunds of excavation creating the high-level plateaus. The site was covered in 150mm of crushed concrete as a defence against illegal vehicle entry to the Thames Barrier.

The areas surrounding the site formed an ever-changing industrial backdrop – the nearby Tate and Lyle building bringing in cargo ships to their dockside refinery, next door a working scrapyard piled high with rusting metal, to the west of the site an oil refinery and to the north the remnants of Ronan Point, which was being demolished.

As well as making urban connections with this backdrop and the future expansion plans for the Docklands, we had to invent a context for the park. It was not a case of simply laying a green carpet over the area. We first cut a slice into the ground to create

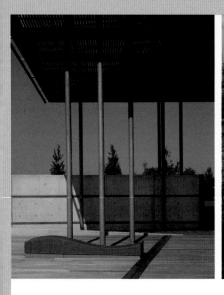

the green dock, which allowed us to level out the low lying plateau areas with the excavated fill. The excavated spoil from the many tree pits was also used for further landscaping and contouring.

The sunken green dock is the machined landscape, cut into the plateau at a diagonal. Within it are fountains and long rows of formal planting flanked by 7m-high concrete retaining walls and traversed by overhead footbridges. The green dock leads to the Pavilion at the river end of the park and to the café and Visitor Centre at the entrance.

The architectural concept was to enclose the whole park and frame it like a composition. The axis of the park allows you to go north and take the new footbridge over North Woolwich Road, which is at park plateau level, and continue towards the Excel Centre. The park plan may appear simple at first, but it is very detailed. There are pathways between the formal rows of tree planting on the plateau and a diagonal path that runs from the north-east corner, crossing the green dock by footbridge to reach the south-west tip of the park facing the river. The 300m-long green dock that cuts into the plateau creates the other axial link tying the spaces together.

The plateau is a 250m square; a kilometre-long walk around the perimeter. The plateau has been planted with meadow grass and silver birch, oak and other specimen trees. All the level changes across the park are made with small or large retaining walls.

The idea of the green dock was to have concrete walls framing the 30m-wide formal planting with its granite paths and fountains. When we were considering the detailing of the paths and retaining walls, we referred to old photographs taken of the original Pontoon Dock. What we liked about it was the robustness of its construction, the sheet piling and the concrete.

The exposed concrete walls were cast with thin horizontal bands of inset granite to break up their flatness. We also added a positive ariss, like the ones that Louis Kahn detailed. Carlo Scarpa is also a recurrent theme in our work, from whom we drew inspiration. We quite like rough cast with smooth surfaces and the contrast of materials.

The next element is the Visitor Centre, which you access via the bridge that picks up the north walkway of the site. How do you solve the problem of a building that incorporates a café, which is all windows, and the toilets, kitchen and storerooms, which have none? Simple – build a concrete box for the kitchen, toilets and storerooms and use green oak for framing the café. The contrast between the two materials echoes the concrete and greenery in the park.

Camden Square Adventure Playground, Peckham
Selina Dix-Hamilton, Eger Architects

At the entrance to the park via the green dock there is a ramp designed as a box culvert where people can circulate and which is used to house the pumping gear for the fountains. In essence, it is a free-standing structure, backfilled in parts.

Along the pontoon edge of the green dock and the perimeter of the park we designed an insitu edge slab rather than precast panels onto which the handrail was bolted. Insitu created a slightly weathered, coarser finish which was more like stone. The pathway along the top edge of the green dock was sand blasted and the handrail section left smooth. On leaving the green dock we introduced granite banding into the concrete walls to mimic the ground level contours as you walk towards the Pavilion and waterfront.

The Pavilion canopy is 7m high and supported on slender steel hollow sections in a random pattern, which was quite complicated to analyse structurally. On the river front there is a gravel pathway which is bonded together with resin. The balustrades are cast iron with stainless steel handrails. These become hardwood handrails as they continue back into the park.

The topography of this compact park is derived from the way dunes are formed around an oasis, encouraging imaginative play and providing natural separations between the different activity areas.

The park is extensively planted, bringing a new greenness to the area. In contrast, the perimeter is clearly defined by a wall, which rises and sinks in relation to the pavement, creating a hard urban edge.

The young people who were consulted in the area wanted a park that was like nobody else's. They always showed palm trees in the models they made and, after further discussion with them, we hit on the idea of creating a dunescape. The site was completely level so we had the opportunity, using cut and fill, to make dune-like contours over certain areas. Young people like climbing on roofs – that's usually where all the trouble begins – so we thought we should make the roof of the indoor sports hall accessible to them. So the building was integrated into the landscape and was evolved into a free-form shape, which particularly suited the use of concrete.

Another reason for using concrete was to build a very robust building. One side of the building is alongside a public pavement and will undoubtedly receive quite a lot of abuse. The interior of the building has to be durable and hard wearing.

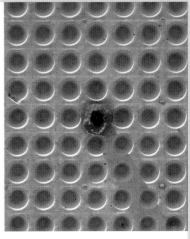

The park houses various play areas for different activities and different age groups. Some features are for less-able people and there is a small garden with play equipment for toddlers who are less than five years of age. On the roof of the building there are swings and a giant slide that goes down the slope of the roof, which is a spectacular attraction visible from
far away.

Inside the building we have a climbing wall 7.5m high which gives the form to our building structure. The climbing wall was introduced by the client half way through the project so the hill of our building became considerably steeper and the slide considerably more exciting.

The plot size is 50 × 100m and the building occupies a rectangular space along one side of the park. The building is 25m long and has a triangular elevation with the apex 8m above ground level. The giant slope that the slide sits on and the surround to the slate bowl is on a soil bank built up over the building. Inside the building there is a hall containing the climbing wall and floor area for general use by young people. It has a stainless steel curtain that protects and covers the climbing wall when it is not in use. The curtain can either be pegged out to fixings in

the floor to divide the space or fixed to the climbing wall to protect it. There is an office for the chief play officer and a bigger office which can take up to eight young people, where they can create a magazine and organise events. The main door on the street side will allow the hall to be used by the public at night or let to local organisations. The young people always wished for an adult to be on hand to have the playground supervised. Other adults will only be allowed into the facility if they have a young person with them.

There is a lot of bold planting, as well as seven large palm trees. The landscape design concept is that the dunes naturally separate the zoned areas and eliminate the need to screen the skateboard bowl from the main pathway. The stripes on the grass, achieved by planting two different coloured grasses in bands, simulate the movement and wind that create dunes. We carried that idea through to the resin floor inside the building and coloured it red and orange, as young people like bright colours.

Scharnhauser Park, Ostfildern, Germany
Alban Janson, Janson and Wolfrum Architects, Stuttgart

Public buildings and residential apartment blocks line the long green landscaped carpet on either side, like a racecourse. The stepped terraced grassland is a huge land drain and forms the spine of the entire development, enclosing the centre within a slight curvature until it reaches the open fields.

The landscape concept was to create a central terraced grassy slope that was 40m wide and 1km long, running like a green spine through the middle of the new conurbation of Ostfildern. The drop was only 20m, or a gradient of 2% over 1,000m, which really does not warrant a staircase but we liked it for architectural reasons and to create drainage lagoons. The slope would hardly be noticeable without the stepped terraces breaking the green spaces at intervals along its length. We wanted to show the slope and not the flatness of the ground and this was one way of doing it. From the top of the slope looking down, it's a green carpet cutting through the new town; from the bottom of the slope looking up, it's a solid wall of stepped terracing.

All the rainwater from the nearby estate roads and apartment roofs is piped to flow into the shallow hollows of the grassy slopes between the terraces to become temporary rainwater lagoons during prolonged rainfall. The grassy hollows fill from the highest level and any surcharge spills over the notch in the lower terrace to gently cascade into the next grassy hollow. The grassy hollows are soakaways that eventually drain the lagoons when the storm has passed and they return to being grass-covered slopes once again. This was a very pleasing and environmentally friendly way of disposing of the surface water. We had a civil engineer who designed the drainage system. It's delightful to see children playing in the shallow lagoons after a storm, floating their boats or just paddling.

We choose white precast concrete for the terrace steps, the culverts and rainwater interceptors and sidewalks. It was inexpensive, durable and resembled marble. There was an option to use grey paving slabs, but white is a better contrast with green. We referred to it as reconstructed stone to avoid the negative reception that concrete often receives from the public. No one to this day has realised that it is concrete. We also imported some large boulders of marble and placed them along the sidewalks near the terraces and in some ways this reinforces the suggestion that the precast paving slabs are marble.

The central channel with the notched steps on the terraces has radial marks to help improve grip and slip resistance. Most of the time the steps are dry and it is a surface feature. The choice of grass has

been a major exercise in selection. Expert advice was sought from the turf and sports industries. There are three different grass seeds in the mixture to create a hard wearing, drought-resistant covering that would be quick to recover. The grass is trimmed once a month to keep it short, otherwise it will overgrow the steps. Sheep also graze along the slope to help keep it trim.

At the top of the slope that leads to the new tram station there is a paved arbour of walnut trees with a children's play area, a network of drainage channels and rows of low-level lights. This formal piazza with flowering trees looks down the long landscaped stairway. Along the sides of the green slope there are newly planted deciduous trees which will grow to screen the hard edges of the apartment blocks that fringe the verdant pasture.

In the bleak winter when the ground is covered in snow and you can't see much of the terraces it is still enjoyable to walk the kilometre. We have a saying in our office for such occasions, that although there may be little to view there is much to experience! It's a gentle climb for ski walking in winter, a running track for joggers, a pleasant stroll in summer and a place to sit and watch the sun go down over the Swabian mountains.

CONCRETE ELEGANCE//
03THE TACTILE FAÇADE

The Tactile Façade
Visually Sensitive Architecture

Wiel Arets, Wiel Arets Architects, Maastricht
Manuelle Gautrand, Manuelle Gautrand Architects, Paris

Concrete can be designed as a screen wall, a sculpture and a façade, to diffuse harmful sunlight from light-sensitive books and to form a ribbon structure for a vast conference room. Innovation and sensory perception best describe such architecture.

The fabric façade: University Library, Utrecht

Wiel Arets, Wiel Arets Architects

In any library, the storage of books and other light-sensitive items requires closed spaces, while the study space for students and researchers requires openness. This project's organisation of spaces seeks to reconcile the paradoxical requirements of a university library in an ingenious manner. The closed volumes of the storage areas are suspended like opaque clouds in the air, yet the open structure gives visitors an experience of spaciousness and freedom. Patterns are printed onto the glazing and the concrete façades to create the sense of a building in the woods and to reduce sunlight penetration.

The glass façade also encloses the car park like a smooth skin, making it an integral part of the complex. On one side is the university site, where the view from the raw interior offers a filtered prospect of the open countryside surrounding it; on the other side there is the view of the long slopes situated beside the inner courtyard that work as blinds to filter the view of the car park. In the double panelled curtain wall there are window openings for the management and research staff.

When we designed the building we had the idea of casting two black concrete panels hanging in space like two black clouds. Seen externally, the black panels are the solid part of the façade. Where they are imprinted with bamboo-like motifs they signal the book depots, where they are plain and smooth they frame or enclose a plant room, meeting rooms or a service zone. The concrete panels internally are perforated by openings for the bridge links that allow access to other parts of the building. Silent communication is important in a library where talking is kept to a minimum. The atmosphere is determined by an emphasis on noise reduction surfaces. It was essential to select a dark interior colour to set the mood.

The library is more than a place where people can consult books – it is a place where they can work in a concentrated fashion, and also one where they can meet other people without the need for any other stimuli except the atmosphere that the building radiates. The storage areas or book depots, which seem to float like clouds, divide the space into zones and are interconnected by stairs and slopes. The book depots, in black figured concrete and on which the reading rooms rest, are encased by a double-glazed façade, to which a silk screen design has been applied in order to let natural light into the building.

A shiny white floor and desk tops provide enough reflection of natural or artificial light to illuminate some of the 42 million books that are on open shelves, while the long white tables make it possible

to read a book or to consult electronic information without too much effort. The individual workplaces, each with full facilities, are the key elements, and have been positioned in such a way that the user's choice of a workplace also determines their degree of communication with other users.

Absorption versus confrontation, silent study versus verbal communication – this is the main premise of this library, whose infrastructure has more than one function. The architecture must respond to this programme. We have created meeting, talking, greeting spaces like the bar, the lounge area, the reception corner, the auditorium, and fitted them with sound-absorbing red rubber floors and panels. Other elements such as the shops and atrium add an extra dimension, breaking down the mono-functionality of the library programme.

Tactile concrete architecture
Manuelle Gautrand, Manuelle Gautrand Architects

The three projects highlighted have a close relationship with the environment and draw inspiration from nature and simple everyday materials.

In the A16 Toll Booths in northern France, for example, we wanted to think about the landscape and the region's historical context. The motorway is located in an unspoilt region of the countryside. We were keen to find some uplifting and sensitive design that would soften the impact of the toll stations on the surrounding landscape and also please the motorist. We were inspired by the different landscapes along the route – the blue flowers of linseed oil cultivation, the blue of the sea, the yellow flowers of the rapeseed, the red poppies in the fields, the green leaves of the trees and shrubs of the woodlands and planting on the embankments of the roadway. The other inspirational idea was the use of stained glass, for which this region is famous.

We decided to place the administrative buildings and plant rooms behind a screen wall to hide them from view and to create a wind-break. This separation gave the administrative building and service facilities their own space and did not corrupt the openness and clarity of the canopy area. The screen wall panels were precast concrete, pigmented in the primary colours of the canopy motif although not an exact match. The blue became a shiny dark purple-grey, the red was more a maroon, the yellow was ochre, and so on. They stretch the length of the toll area and turn through right angles to corral the administrative buildings on three sides. On the 5m-high precast panels we have imprinted the profile of the branches of shrubs and trees that we see in the distant fields. The precast panels represent the landscape and are covered with vegetation imprints that thin out towards the top.

We chose five colours for the glass laminate canopies – blue, red, yellow, pale green and mid-green – one for each toll station. For the red patterns we designed large poppy images in red in a random arrangement, as if it had rained poppies on the canopy. For blue it was the linseed flower, for pale green it was maple leaves, for mid-green it was ivy leaves and for yellow it was the rapeseed flower. This creates wonderful light patterns and colours passing over the traffic below.

For the Lille Museum of Modern Art the key for our approach lies in what may appear to be a detail of secondary importance in the programme brief. With the construction of the new west wing, the suggestion was made to create a technical link to the north, along the patio wall, so as to connect the new extension and the two existing wings to improve functional shortcomings in the present museum. We used this suggestion to the full, using the boundary of the existing wing as the interface to attach the new building to, making available complex curving volumes that develop freely along this angular boundary edge. In a single movement, the most diverse components within the new building and the existing areas were merged into an arrangement that was coherent.

This approach effectively avoids entering into a conflict with the existing building and also solves practical problems. The extension, being of comparable length as it wraps itself along the back of the existing building, is perceived by visitors as being complementary to the existing architecture. Its formal expression is not related to any building style and is dominated by what already exists.

Four basic characteristics explain the distribution of the project. First, the west part of the extension, which is mainly technical, is occupied by a café that faces south onto the central patio. This option unifies the relations between the enlarged entrance hall towards the patio, the bookshop and the new cafeteria. Second, the junction with the exhibition rooms simplifies the 'backstage' technical work, with the possibility of isolating them without hampering the museum visit. Third, the new rooms for the main exhibition area and temporary exhibitions are laid out logically with the rest of the museum complex. Fourth and last, the approach uses the existing building grid pattern. The exhibition rooms, named the Art Brut rooms, are designed as spaces that are connected by their physical contouring to the soil and to the plants that will partially cover the fine filigree external concrete screen walls that have been conceived in white Ductal. The sparse natural light that is allowed in demands an architecture that is introverted.

The Concrete Flower Project on the other hand is bold and extrovert in concept. It is being designed for an international industrial group looking to build a high-profile reception facility for visitors. Design-wise, the objective was to imagine a single, centrally located facility for the site; one that will serve to

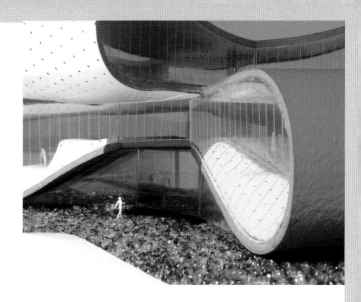

welcome, inform, orient, exhibit and communicate, while guiding visitors to their appointments, meeting rooms or work places. Underlying this was the client's wish to create a service building that was striking not only due to the efficient reception but also to the spatial and aesthetic qualities of its architecture: it aims to give people an unforgettable architectural experience.

We began by imagining a concentric arrangement of spaces, defined by a huge ribbon tied around a parcel, to express the feeling of welcome. The structure works like a revolving platform, drawing in and distributing the flow of visitors, who pass by the reception before continuing on their journeys.

We needed to find the most appropriate form to enable us to pull all the spaces together, and the result is a simple radiating sculpture formed of three ribbon loops at ground level, with three slightly smaller ribbon loops set above them. Seen in plan it is a flower, with two superposed tiers of alternating petals. All the ribbon loops are made in precast concrete, with the lower tier folded downwards and the upper tier folded upwards.

Together, the six loops form a sculptured structure

that opens between the two existing buildings and whose figure enlivens the context by its formal liberty, sensual curves, aerial presence and complex function. The loops are encased by full-height clear glass side walls. Each loop encloses a distinct element of the programme that is easily identifiable for the public.

The lower tier integrates a large auditorium, conference rooms and an introductory exhibition space. The upper tier houses the VIP reception area (salon and restaurant) and any follow-on exhibition space.

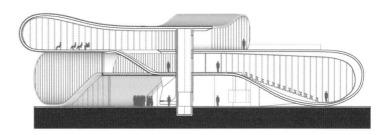

CONCRETE ELEGANCE// 04FIREBOWLS AND GEOTEXTILE CONCRETE

Firebowls and Geotextile Concrete
Christian Van Outersterp, CVO Ltd
Remo Pedreschi, University of Edinburgh

Innovative ideas in concrete using hand-made concrete firebowls for heating a home and fabric-formed shapes for low cost, load-bearing elements.

CVO firebowls

Christian Van Outersterp, CVO Ltd

CVO introduced an innovative firebowl for burning fossil fuel or Ceramat – a man-made material that does not burn conventionally but produces ripples of gas flames that float on the firebowl like a fluid. The bowl is made from polished GRC, in a rounded organic shape that comes with a black or white finish.

The firebowl is precast on a specially formed mould. The wet mix of GRC is hand-sprayed in layers over the mould to the required thickness. It is then polished to a fine ceramic smoothness when hardened. The GRC for a white firebowl comprises white cement, fine white limestone sand and small aggregates, mixed with glass fibre strands. For the black firebowl a black sand and black pigment is added to the mix. The firebowls are made in a factory in Yorkshire and come in two sizes and two shapes – circular and oval.

The small, 400mm-long oval has an output of 9.3 kilowatts (kW), the larger 70mm oval gives 16.2kW and the circular 490mm bowl also gives 16.2kW.

A cast aluminium tray sits in the firebowl to contain the Ceramat fuel. This is a non-combustible

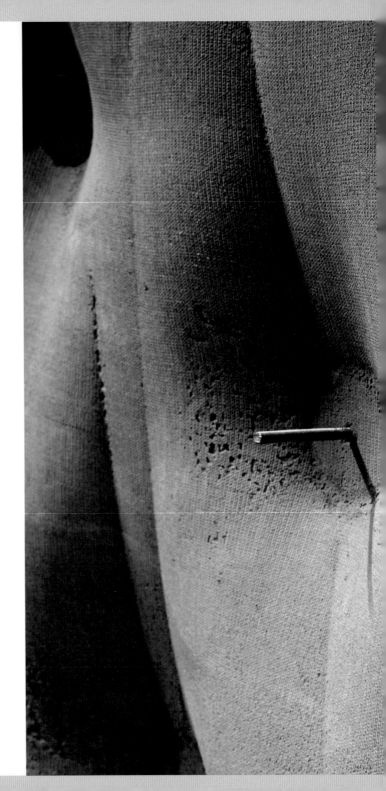

material made of tiny glass fibre tubes coated with graphite that was developed by NASA for the outer skin protection of the Space Shuttle. When the gas is ignited, the Ceramat draws the gas flames through its tubes and spreads the flame evenly over the suface, where it burns with a clean, blue colour.

An 8mm gas feed is connected to the base of the firebowl, which can be supplied with either an electrical infra red ignition or a manual ignition. The firebowl flame has very low emissions, in some cases half the CO and CO_2 of coal-effect gas fires at half the kilowatt output. It will still require an enclosed flue or an extractor flue if it sits in an open area.

Advantages of using a concrete firebowl are that it does not become too hot on the outside and is safe to the touch and it is easy to keep clean with soap and water. The Ceramat fuel has a life of ten years and must be changed after this time in order to keep the gas flame working effectively.

Studies in fabric-formed concrete

Remo Pedreschi, University of Edinburgh

Fabric-formed concrete involves casting concrete in a framework or canvas made with flexible fabrics. By careful shaping of the fabric it is possible to produce complex shapes that would otherwise be difficult to manufacture using conventional formwork systems. The permeability of the fabric assists curing and reduces surface defects. The surface finish follows the texture of the fabric. Fabric casting can produce elements that are structurally efficient and visually dramatic in a relatively inexpensive and practical manner.

My interest in fabric-formed concrete began some years ago when I first met Mark West at a conference in Montevideo. Since that time there has been collaboration between Mark West at Manitoba University and our team at Edinburgh University. The work that we have researched and piloted has been in improving shape forming and stitching techniques, making joint connections work really well and developing concrete mixes for specific fabric forms and applications. Our interest has been in component assembly and ensuring consistency and predictability in the construction process. The objective of this work has been student-based learning and research. It's not a full-time project as yet and occupies a short five-week period in the final year of the architecture degree course. However, we hope that in time the results from this work will provide the construction approach, fabric specification and overall methodology to be able to build and test structures that have been designed on the drawing board. The overall aim is to transfer the technology to the construction industry with the appropriate design rules and performance standards in place.

The most useful fabrics for this form of construction are engineered geotextiles made from durable synthetic polymers or polypropylene. Geotextiles have been developed for temporary and permanent road construction to maintain the integrity of the granular sub-base layer by reducing intermixing with the formation and allowing water to filter through while minimising heave and depression of the formation under the action of wheel loads. Such a geotextile will have a known tensile strength, elongation limit, pore size, water permeability and puncture resistance and can be supplied in different grades. They are usually 1–3mm in thickness and are either woven or non-woven. We have also used Lycra and hessian.

We have incorporated such fabrics in the research project that the students can choose in their third year. The architecture students, working in teams

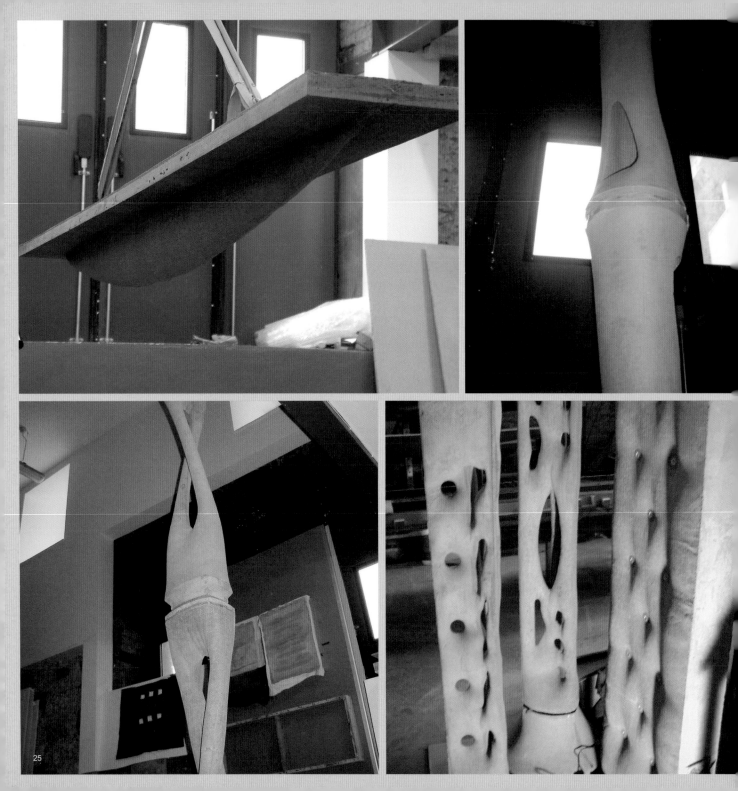

of three or four, are given five weeks to design a shape, or a component part of an overall structure or a joint connection. In the first week they sketch their ideas, in the next few weeks they make trial castings of sections to learn the techniques of fabric stitching, concrete mixing and placing, vibration and compaction and how to maintain the shape and profile of this very stretchy and flexible material. To control the shape, wooden templates are used and the fabric is tensioned with clamps and ties as necessary. The fabric has to be framed in a supporting or backing structure so that the assembly is rigid and will not collapse or topple over, or cause the stitches to rupture during concreting. In the final week they build the prototype that they designed and give a presentation to document what they have done and how it was achieved. The presentation documents are retained by the department and used as background information from which the next year's students can learn. The programme has been running for two years and the results are phenomenal.

We now have a PhD student working on the analysis of form-active fabric beams. The beam takes the shape of the bending moment curve for a distributed load that is simply supported; therefore they are called form-active. The research will also investigate the end bearing and end connection detail, which currently tapers to a thick, flat concrete flange.

By requiring less material than conventional concrete, this technique promises significant reductions in embodied energy, material cost and transport weight. Fabric-formed concrete can be used to make columns, wall panels, slabs and beams for both cast-in-place and precast applications. And once the structural analysis and testing have been completed, we are sure it will prove to be a viable method of construction worldwide. Moreover, such a material is rich in aesthetic possibilities and offers an almost unlimited palette for free-form design in architecture and engineering.

Materials and Form
Raw Edged or Refined Smoothness?
William Russell, William Russell Architects
Sheila O'Donnell and John Toumey, O'Donnell Toumey Architects

Insitu concrete can be made to look as smooth as porcelain with painstaking effort and care or cast with the rawness of the shutter using the average skills of a local builder. Both forms will impact on the ambience of the space they enclose and the style of architecture they create.

23–25 Bacon Street, London

William Russell, William Russell Architects

We had no intention of building our own home, although it's the dream of every architect. Together with Sheila Muiry, my partner who is an architect with her own practice, I was looking for a run-down terrace house to renovate and refurbish. At every auction we went to, the properties that we were bidding for sold for more than we were prepared to pay. And then we found this untidy site not far from my office in Brick Lane. The auction notice had fallen over and lay on a pile of rubbish. We took the details down. The site was small and dirty and was being used for parking a few cars and collecting unwanted rubbish. Next door was the school of St Matthias, and the other side of the road was wasteland. The car park was enclosed by sheets of rusty corrugated iron.

The auction took place in an upstairs room in the Design Centre in Islington. It was August, it was quiet and we were lucky as the usual crowd of builders that attend these gatherings were away on their summer holidays. We bought it for less than we had budgeted. Then we spent the next two years designing our dream home, obtaining planning permission and finding a contractor to build it. It had to be concrete – it was honest, reassuringly solid, durable and secure. Designing a home for your own family is primeval and you want

to make it a shelter that is strong and protective – a cave of concrete in fact. There were outside influences on our design ideas but we wanted to build it our way, to evolve the space plan from our hearts and minds.

The building has been divided temporarily into two living accommodations. The basement and ground floor has been made into a self-contained apartment, which is rented out. The basement flat is naturally lit from the glass on the front elevation and back light from the glazed light well down the side of the house. Later, the flat will revert back into the family home when the children get older and need separate bedrooms. At present they share. The first and second floors are reached by a narrow concrete staircase leading from the ground floor. At first floor level are two bedrooms, one of which is the master bedroom, and the bathroom. The large light-filled double height second floor space contains the main living area, the kitchen and dining rooms. There is also a roof terrace with a bathroom and balustrade that overlooks the second floor. In many ways this house is like living in a concrete castle with its narrow winding staircase.

The concrete contractors were Tom and Martin who were recommended to me by Nick

Hanniker of Price and Myers. The school next door very generously allowed us to use part of the playground for the site huts and to store construction material. Once the basement had been excavated and the piles and pile caps had been cast, the concrete superstructure progressed.

We did not specify any special form face material, nor issue the contractor with a cutting plan showing the tie bolt hole locations or the pour sequence. Even though the concrete cover spacers were laid flat and you can see the dog bone outline on the ceilings, the concrete finish was smooth and quite acceptable. It was not meant to be precious, it had a stone-like quality, which was mottled and patchy in colour, but it was monolithic, hard and natural. Perhaps the rawness was more pronounced on the staircase balustrade which, at only 70mm thick, was very difficult to form. The overall effect has the look of well worn leather, with a depth of colour and warmth that you would not get from the synthetic tint of a coat of paint or a skim of plaster.

The floors in the living rooms and bedrooms have under-floor heating, so a topping concrete was poured later, which was floated and then ground smooth with a carborundum disc. The polished kitchen worktop is a heavily reinforced insitu

concrete slab 125mm thick, which cantilevers from the perimeter concrete wall.

The external cladding wraps itself around the concrete structure. From second floor dado to the roof it's a wrap of white laminated double glazing units which allow in generous amounts of natural daylight whilst affording privacy. There is a double height sliding window panel on the street elevation to the south, which opens to allow in bags of fresh air. Galvanised panels with flame retardant insulation wrap around the elevation from ground floor to second floor, on three sides of the building. There are window penetrations for the bedrooms and shower room on the first floor. The roof and the north elevation, or back of the building, are heavily insulated and clad in a skin of black rubberised membrane called Evalon, made of Eva-Terpolymer, which is tough and durable.

Plywood fittings, designer lights and furniture in the living spaces add contrast and interest against the calm concrete backdrop to make this house a real dream home for the Russell family.

Cherry Orchard Primary School, Dublin
Sheila O'Donnell, O'Donnell Tuomey Architects

The brief for this new national school was non-standard. It was developed in consultation with the Department of Education and Science, Cherry Orchard Parish Priests and their advisers. The social conditions in this area of Dublin led to the inclusion of special facilities for pre-school children, children with special needs and facilities for the care of children outside school hours, and it is the first school of its kind in Ireland to include this broad range of functions. These special functions required the inclusion of a pre-school nursery, a special care unit, an early start centre, a home-school liaison room and a number of multipurpose rooms for teaching special needs pupils, as well as general catering facilities.

The predominant feeling in this part of Cherry Orchard is one of anonymity or lack of identity. The challenge was to find a design solution that would give the school a strong identity and, to an extent, create its own context, a context that would be welcoming and attractive for pupils from all backgrounds, including the most socially deprived.

The scheme takes the form of a school within a walled garden planted with a cherry orchard. The school is arranged between a series of courtyards within a 3.6m-high brick garden wall. The brick wall

provides shelter and protection to the school and the outdoor play areas, while giving the building a strong architectural form on the site. All of the accommodation is two storeys high and leads onto the garden-playgrounds.

The rooms take their light from the courtyards. The perimeter walls are generally without openings, except for the main entrance, the rear entrance to the ball court play area and a number of openings which give low level views into and out of the gardens. The walls establish the character of the gardens. The height of the garden walls has been carefully gauged to allow the trees to be visible above the walls from the outside.

The concept of the walled garden is central to the project and provides a strong sense of place while also affording a degree of shelter. The three building elements – brick walls, vaulted concrete roofs and hardwood finishes – form a palette of materials which are robust but which will weather naturally and give the building a sense of being rooted in its site.

Tonality and Patination
Natural and Synthetic Coloured Concrete

Nick Lee, Greenway and Lee Architects
Jochen Glemser, David Chipperfield Architects

In the world of concrete today we can choose to be extrovert colourists or cool purists when it comes to selecting the tonality of concrete.
We can consider how best to achieve consistence in pigmented concrete, ensure an even surface colour where required, and enhance vibrancy of concrete.

Spedant Works, London

Nick Lee, Greenway and Lee Architects

The building occupies a footprint of 4,700ft^2 or 11 × 20m and to the ridge has a height of 9m. The project was to create a new workspace for stained-glass artist Brian Clarke, incorporating an office, a design studio and a display area for making presentations to clients. The initial brief was to keep the existing studio and refurbish it, but after a fuller appraisal we convinced him that it would be better to knock down the studio and rebuild a new one more suited to his current and future needs.

As it is a working studio we decided the floors should be power-floated concrete with a hard wearing industrial finish. It would take a lot of wear and tear and could be cleaned quite easily. We then introduced a contrasting palette of materials, with smooth floors, board-marked concrete walls and painted white plasterboard. The board-marked idea came from our many visits to Switzerland, where my family live and where concrete is used to great effect, and from Denys Lasdun's architecture, which I studied as an undergraduate.

On the main elevation we designed a protruding window box at first floor level, which breaks out from the façade line. We cast it in the same board-marked concrete to give a hint at what's happening inside the building.

By introducing full height glass panels to the sides we created a projecting bay in which to sit and reflect and which also allows a view of the entrance from the first floor.

We specified solid pieces of 18mm-thick Douglas fir slats for the board marking from a timber merchant in South London. The width was chosen so that it worked into the height of the wall without any half cuts. Douglas fir has knots and a graininess to it that makes a wonderful imprint on the concrete surface; the effect is sublime. We specified a high-quality birch ply for the soffits which we recycled for back shuttering in forming the board-marked balustrade walls and the external wall on the first floor. We also used the panels for making the underside of the tabletops and worktops and for backing to the birch ply staircase. The Douglas fir slats were salvaged and used for garden decking so there was no wastage.

Materials were kept to a basic palette of concrete, painted plasterboard and birch ply. The ceilings, brickwork and the blockwork walls were rendered and painted white, as was the exposed steelwork to the first floor. Furniture units – shelving, worktops, benches and storage – were made from birch ply. The staircase design idea was to have solid board-marked concrete walls and between them lightweight birch ply stair treads and no riser so you can see straight through.

On the ground floor adjoining the loading bay there is a floating partition which is closed off to keep the work area separate from the loading dock and at other times it can be opened for material handling. Part of the sliding partition also hides a storage area behind the staircase so that it is not visible when you come in via the main entrance. The sliding panels are 3.5m high and are all painted white for use in presentations.

Villaverde Housing Project, Madrid
Jochen Glemser, David Chipperfield Architects

Commissioned by the Empresa Municipal de la Vivienda (EMV), the social housing scheme is located on a new development in Verona, in the Villaverde district of southern Madrid. It comprises 176 one-, two- and three-bedroom apartments. The scheme responds to the overall master plan for the site, which required a large single U-shaped block, 15m deep and with a footprint of just over 2,000m². Like other buildings within the same development, it also required the block to be eight stories high and have a pitched roof.

Within the confines of this brief, the design attempted to manipulate these architectural restrictions so as to abstract the common idea of an apartment block. Whereas other neighbouring buildings adopt a symmetrical, double-pitched silhouette, here the traditional relationships of wall and roof are abstracted into a low, single pitch for the bulk of the block, and a minimal secondary pitch that bevels the front edge of the building. The increase in floor area achieved by this allowed for a more sculptural approach to the building envelope, carving the sides of the block away from the orthogonal, to create a more varied outline to the building elevations.

The detailing of the façade sections with their reveals, corner closures, differing panel sizes and colour tone was an attempt to liberate the solid mass of the building. The façade is not a rain screen, it's a sealed system with silicone weather-tight joints. The GRC panels, which are 20–25mm thick and span between floors, wrap around the deep window recesses and narrow balcony slots. The units are arranged in different modular sizes, and have been pigmented with slightly more or less terracotta pigment to emphasise the patination that often occurs with pigmented concrete. The supporting frame is an insitu concrete flat slab with rectangular columns and shear walls. The location of the columns grid, the stair core and the distribution of the apartments over the eight floors influence the façade's geometric rhythm.

This three-dimensional study into mass and form also represents a two-dimensional, almost mathematical exercise in colour patterning. The subtle changes in pigment tone and concrete patination are not seen as a negative characteristic but blend in with the overall pixellated appearance of the building. In many ways it breaks down the heavy monumental appearance that a uniform colour would have given.

City of Justice Buildings, Barcelona
Jochen Glemser, David Chipperfield Architects

The various legal departments of the governments of Barcelona and l'Hospitalet were scattered in seventeen buildings across the two cities, with administrative frustrations for both users and employees. New conjoined City of Justice buildings were commissioned to improve efficiency, to adapt and absorb the constant transformation of the judicial body, as well as provide space for future growth.

The site is at the border of the two cities of Barcelona and l'Hospitalet and located adjacent to both Gran Via, a major access route into the centre of Barcelona from the south, and Carrilet, an artery leading to l'Hospitalet. The position provides optimum accessibility to the city and major metropolitan routes, on both public and private transport.

The proposed design of the project breaks down the massive programme requirements (330,000m^2) into a series of separate but interrelated blocks. This spatial composition attempts to overcome the rigid and monolithic image of justice. The proposal also attempts to provide equilibrium to the relationships between the different working areas, public areas and landscape.

A group of four large judicial buildings is situated around the perimeter of a linking concourse building.

The buildings generally contain courtrooms at ground floor level and on a further three floors. All of these floors are accessed directly from the concourse building, which acts as a filter. The concourse building also gathers people at the start and completion of their judicial visit within a central public room overlooking the exterior plaza.

Four other independent buildings comprise a judicial services building for l'Hospitalet, a forensic sciences building and two commercial buildings with retail facilities at ground floor level. A further building is planned to contain both residential and commercial retail activities.

All eight buildings are conceived as formally restrained blocks, each with a unique coloured load-bearing façade. Each building has a different but muted colour tone. The concourse building has a more free-form plan with deep exposed concrete slabs and woven mesh screens in front of frameless glazing.

Many façade options in metal, brick, stone and concrete were considered and assessed before we made our choice. Concrete was preferred and further investigations on the insitu or precast alternatives were analysed. The final decision was

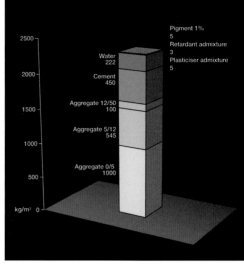

taken in favour of insitu concrete. Next we had to develop the concrete specification and the design of a load-bearing façade that would tie into the frame without causing cold bridging problems. The concrete specified was a self-compacting mix that was to be batched on site with the greatest of care. A concrete batching plant was installed on site with covered bins and silos for this purpose. Concrete would be transported to the various buildings using truck mixer and concrete pumping equipment.

Samples were made to assess colour stability and surface tone using different pigment concentrations made with grey and white cements. We worked with Lanxess who manufacture Bayferrox pigments and sought their advice on the colour blends that we required. We did consider the options of natural coloured fine aggregates but the colour range was too limited for our purposes. Full-scale mock-ups for each building colour were carried out and then repeated to ensure that the colour was uniform for each batch and did not patinate. The requirements for this project were the opposite to those on the Villaverde project in Madrid, where we expected patination. The high percentage of fines in the self-compacting mix and the low pigment concentration of between 1 and 2 per cent created a subdued pastel colour that was very consistent and did not patinate.

Metal faced formwork was used to give the texture and surface quality of the finish on the façade. The formwork was used many times and produced a high-quality finish as a result of careful cleaning and preparation before every pour. The release agent was tested to avoid any discolouration of the surface. To prevent any staining from grout runs when the upper panels were being poured, the lower panels were washed down during the pour.

The prefabricated metal façade formwork allowed construction to rise at a floor a month. With four sets in use, one set for each building, the four large coloured concrete buildings were topped out in eight months.

CONCRETE ELEGANCE//
07THE MILLAU VIADUCT

The Millau Viaduct
A Towering Achievement
Alistair Lenczner, Foster and Partners
Russell Stanley, PERI Ltd

One of finest bridges to be built in the world has become a landmark for establishing so many records. We celebrate the challenge of how the tallest piers in the world, which rise over 300m above the Tarn Gorge, were aesthetically modelled and built.

The cable stayed solution
Alistair Lenczner, Foster and Partners

After the five bridge design proposals for Millau were reviewed by the judging panel chaired by Jean-François Coste, the winning design was confirmed as the cable stayed solution. The cable stayed solution gave the best balance for height, scale and construction economy and made the least visual impact across the wide sloping valley. Working closely with our civil engineering partners we evaluated and contrasted the aesthetics of the various bridging options.

The aesthetic modelling helped to determine the spacing of the spans, the number of piers and their profile. We started with a beam and post idea or box girder bridge concept and concluded the study with our reasons for the cable stayed option.

The crossing is not only that of the river Tarn, which is quite narrow, or between the plateaus on either side of the valley, it is also about the scale of the whole site. The very wide expanse of the valley and the length of the crossing suggested a very even distribution of the piers with minimal visual impact on the skyline. We began by modelling the most economical engineering solution of a box girder deck supported on piers, which resulted in equal spans of 170m. This gave the scheme fourteen pier supports, which would be difficult to

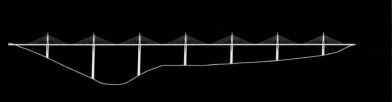

excavate along the varying geology and slope of the valley. Moreover, the massing of the piers and their close centres formed a visual barrier in the landscape that was too intrusive.

By pushing the spans to their limit for a box girder deck, it was possible to increase the span to 260m. In doing so the bridge deck became very deep and transmitted larger wind forces and bending stresses to the supporting piers. The piers therefore had to be stiffened and enlarged and were not very slender. This was aesthetically displeasing.

In order to reduce the bridge deck thickness and the lateral wind forces, while maintaining a 260m or larger span with fewer piers, we next considered the cable stayed solution. Cable stayed bridges are well suited to spans ranging from 250m to 500m without much increase in the bridge deck thickness. A series of 350m spans was considered the optimum spacing for the bridge, which stretches 2.4km across the Tarn valley. The resulting seven slender piers also respect the site topography and make for an economical structural solution with the minimum of visual impact.

However, under the effect of the anticipated temperature variations, a bridge deck of 2.4km expands and contracts with a displacement at the ends of the structure of up to 1m. In order to limit

the displacement on the piers, sliding bearings were placed between the deck and the piers. The piers had to be designed to be flexible enough to allow this movement to occur if they were to remain slender. In addition, the top part of the piers below the bridge deck had to be flexible to reduce any large bending forces from the frictional resistance of the bearings. At the base, the piers are designed as a solid rigid structure. They then taper in profile as they rise and transform into a splayed or split pier just below the bridge deck to ensure its upper flexibility.

Conversely, the cable mast head had to be rigid and maintain its shape and equilibrium when the stay forces are pulling against it and trying to bend it. The mast head was made rigid by designing it as an A-frame with two down-stand legs. A harp arrangement of cable stays, which is preferred for engineering reasons and makes the least impact on the skyline, was not workable for the A-frame mast head. The A-frame shape grouped the anchors for the stays in the upper half of the mast. Thus, a fan cable arrangement was chosen, which was consistent with the triangular geometry of the mast head.

The curve plan of the bridge alignment was proposed to eliminate the unpleasant sensation a motorist might experience on arrival at a bridge of this height,

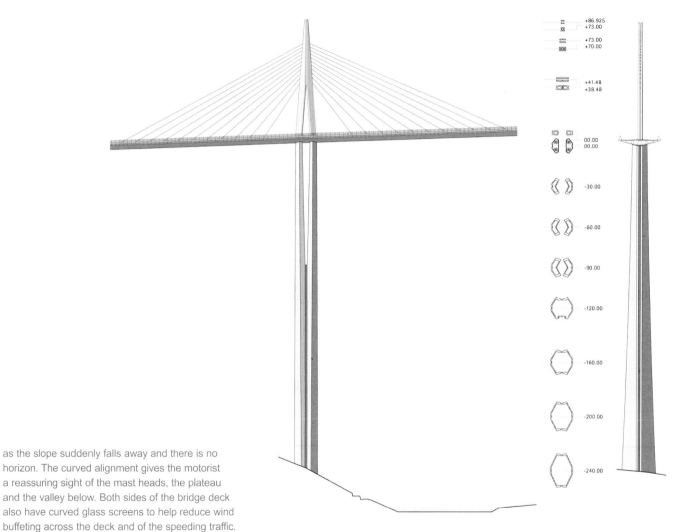

as the slope suddenly falls away and there is no horizon. The curved alignment gives the motorist a reassuring sight of the mast heads, the plateau and the valley below. Both sides of the bridge deck also have curved glass screens to help reduce wind buffeting across the deck and of the speeding traffic.

The built spans are 342m apart, the piers range in height from 75m to 245m with the cable masts rising a further 90m above the road deck. The tapered form of the piers below the bridge deck expresses their structural efficiency and minimises their profile in elevation. The bridge makes a dramatic silhouette on the skyline with the faintest intervention on the landscape.

Forming the piers

Russell Stanley, PERI Ltd

While the pier geometry changed all the way up to the bridge deck, each pier was similar in geometry, which was a great help when designing the adjustable climbing formwork assembly.

Despite the different overall heights of the piers, their profiles were exactly the same from the deck downwards, so that the same climbing formwork scaffold could be used to cast other piers.

The formwork required adjustment for changes in geometry for each lift of 4m. At the base, the tapering pier is 25m long and 17m wide. Just before the pier splits into two halves, 90m below the deck, the pier section reduces in its tapered length to 15m and in width to 16.2m. When the section splits into two halves, the overall length becomes 14.2m and the width 14.7m. The adjustable climbing system also had to climb at an angle of 10° to the vertical.

To adjust the width and length, special 142mm-wide compensation panels were used in combination with telescopic walers that cradle the assembly. After a set number of compensation panels are removed to reduce the section, the telescopic walers pull the assembly together to maintain the altered length and profile.

We used hydraulic pistons, shoe clamps and vertical rails to climb the shutter assembly between lifts.

The system used was the PERI ACS climbing scaffold with integrated working platforms. The system works on the same principle that a caterpillar uses to climb a twig. Using the rail, the piston hydraulically pushes the formwork assembly upwards. The assembly is then clamped in position and the next concrete wall segment is cast. When the forms have to be moved again, the hydraulic piston is moved to the top of the rail which is now at the top of the cast wall. It then pushes the assembly upwards by levering against the clamp toed into the previously cast concrete wall.

Ten climbing scaffold units were used for forming the external skin of the single-shafted pier section and fourteen for the double-shafted piers over the top section. For the inner formwork enclosure of the shaft walls, a self-climbing system could not be used, so crane-assisted climbing units were deployed.

The **Concrete** Centre

The Concrete Centre

Riverside House
4 Meadows Business Park
Station Approach, Blackwater
Camberley, Surrey GU17 9AB

t: 01276 606800

www.concretecentre.com

For free help and advice on the design,
use and performance of concrete, please call
The Concrete Centre's national helpline
on 0700 4 500 500 or 0700 4 CONCRETE

All Concrete Elegance events are free of charge
and take place in The Building Centre in the
evenings. To attend any event or to find out
about current and future programmes, please
contact The Concrete Centre or The Building
Centre Trust.